D1103824

Martin, Let Me Go

Mary Branley

SUMMER PALACE PRESS

First published in 2009 by

Summer Palace Press
Cladnageeragh, Kilbeg, Kilcar, County Donegal, Ireland

Printed by Nicholson & Bass Ltd.

A catalogue record for this book is available
from the British Library

ISBN 978-0-9560995-4-9

This book is printed on elemental chlorine-free paper

For my parents, Padraic and Eileen and especially the niblings,
Paddy, Kitty, and Charlie Bird, Matilda Branley,
my godchild Julia Hanrahan and her new sibling.

Acknowledgments

Some of the poems in this collection have previously appeared in: *Poetry Ireland; Force 10; Cyphers;* and *Europe is a Woman*, an anthology of European Women Poets with Catalan translations, edited by Anna Aguilar-Amat.

Some poems have been broadcast on Ocean FM, on RTE 1 and on Lyric FM.

Biographical Note

Mary Branley's first collection, *A Foot on the Tide*, was published by Summer Palace Press in 2002. Her work has appeared in many journals and anthologies, including *The SHOp*, and most recently the forthcoming *The Watchful Heart* (edited by Joan McBreen for Salmon Publishing 2009). Mary has facilitated creative writing and produced several publications with Kids' Own Publishing Partnership. She has read in various locations in Ireland, London and Colorado, and is a singer-songwriter. She lives in County Sligo and was the recipient of the Sligo County Council Arts Office Residency at the Tyrone Guthrie Centre, Annaghmakerrig. In 2008 she received the Patrick and Katherine Kavanagh Fellowship.

CONTENTS

Martin, let me go

I cannot be the one to save your mother,
though I followed your white coffin to Golgotha,
silent as your cousins
with lager in their hands.
Dying of thirst from all the crying
your mother wanted water,
there was none.

In a broadcast from the halting site,
she named me as friend
and bound me more than any contract could
to an impossible vocation.
But I must know what freedom is
beyond the guilt of privilege,
the duties of the job.

Still you sat behind me in the taxi,
a weightless burden six months on,
as the radio blared your mother's voice again
and my own voice full of June,
though this was Christmas.
You didn't say a word,
as the taxi man announced

My love of fishing takes me out
past Inishmurray, where joyfish dance
and sperm whales play, and I am going
to Tierre Del Fuego in the spring.
Martin, let me go to Tierre Del Fuego
to fish in new waters, away from the bog hole
in which you drowned.

The Plain of Eve

They say
Maugherow
means Plain of Eve

Ballinful,
the town of blood.

Battles,
cattle,
floods.

They say
the ark
shipwrecked
on Beann Gulban,

disgorged
its seasick
passengers
and crew.

They say
if we only knew
the language
we could read

the prayers
written in the sky
by the barnacle geese
as they fly to Inishmurray.

Caravan

Sometimes I sleep with my head in the mountains.
Sometimes I sleep with my feet in the sea.
The applause of rainfall on the trailer wakes me
in the chill of a passionate dawn.
Curved in the oxter of Cloonagh
I thimble the view through the saplings
and dice my day in a single throw.

Wind
for Sue

July

The sea came in under the house
and rocked me, not gently.

The raft in bits and pieces
from the last smash.

Not the ark again
with all those two-by-twos.

The sand-patterned floor
will never need sweeping.

The bladderwrack looks out of place
on the white leather chairs.

I thought a sea wetting did no harm
but the house coughed for days.

August

The wind has peopled the house
with strangers. An angry teen
is banging doors all morning;
the clumsy footfall of a toddler
echoes on wooden floors.
There's a gasp as father ushers in
his restlessness. The kettle clicks.
I lie motionless upstairs.

Barn owls circling
– *scréachóg reilige* –
their prey.

In the briars
a bush vole
whiskers supper.

A hedgehog sups
from a saucer of milk.
I hold my breath.

September

Soft day; I mow the lawn
until stigmata appear
on the palms of both hands

not see-through yet
like Padre Pio's. But

the neighbours know
I won't be cutting
grass again.

October

I curl into the turf wood fire,
can't stay awake.
Stillness is the drug
I take twice daily.

I line the mantelpiece
with candles and mourn
the living.
The house empties out.

November

Winter blanched
the green from fields,
fell soft in deep nights.

The wind sent a bill
for my unpaid debts.

I'm keeping it for
the one who's coming next.

December

The nights keep a beat
to an imagined tune.
Sometimes a chord
of thunder strikes the house,
and wide-eyed, the wind
baffles the fire.

January
I heard the voice again
whispering my name.
Be sensible, my darling,
the poems won't drown, so
I stole these lines from a friend of mine

Pile up more enemies.
Forget your debts.

February

He said a half-starved trout
would leap for my magenta hair.
I watched the sky for signs
until a shark appeared
and followed me home
with a full-moon eye.

March

I closed the door
in every room
and left
the wind
divided into sections
like a cake.

Fridays
for Gerry Burns

Love is back
like the butcher

in his new white van
with hearts for sale

and bones for free.
No questions asked

if you need a line of credit
for two lamb chops,

a bag of mince
and a quarter pound of liver.

Revelations

For a joke in Minnesota
we stripped the deck
of all the lower cards

leaving forty, assigned
each suit a theme,
each card an aspect

of the journey from chaos
to fulfilment.
It was easy. Hearts for love;

spades for work; diamonds, money
and clubs – you'll never guess –
wellbeing. The jacks of course

were wild, a warning of
the unexpected in any suit.
For pregnancy, the nine of hearts.

I don't know why
we hit on that. You pick
nine cards to represent

your life. You'd be surprised
how accurately they show
the misery of work, the poverty
and always, broken hearts.

Copper and Brass

I'm offering you little ...
copper and brass
underfoot in October,
proud mushrooms
on rotting roots
– a colony of fleshed skyscrapers –
edible and poisonous.

I'm offering you little ...
leaves in rags
from cleaning up
the storm,
the jagged edge of an old knife,
a smear of butter
on a slice of bread.

I'm offering you little ...
but I won't burn out
in one fire.
Like seasoned wood
I'll give a soft glow
for hours;
leave useable cinders
in a bed of white ash.

I'm offering you little ...
a glimpse of chaos
behind the calm
and deeper in,
your face etched
on copper and brass
in a loop of perfect sorrow.

Exodus

My mother often threatened
she'd end up across the road
with the fugitives in pyjamas,
bundled into ambulances
outside our house.
Sometimes confused, they'd call
for one of us to ring a taxi
and we would ring for *Them*.

On Sundays, in choir on the altar,
we sang *Reign Lord, oh reign Lord.*
They sang *Faith of Our Fathers*
in fierce rhapsodic counterpoint.
The mad-as-a-hatter chaplain
invited prayers from the faithful
with a roving microphone …

I want to get a job father
Lord hear us.
I want to go home father
Lord hear us.
I want a woman father
Lord hear us.

Outside, patients asked for fags,
pleaded with us *not* to sing for rain.
Once, I saw a nun in full regalia
hitching cars in both directions until she got a lift.
But that was the summer of our discontent,

breakdowns, bankruptcy and night shifts,
when exodus was not that simple.

Father

If I could change the past
I'd take away the cut bare feet;
I'd give you boots and food.

I wouldn't take away your rage.
I'd soften it with butter.
I'd give you an axe and wood to chop
instead of chickens' necks to wring.

So you wouldn't have to cross the icy lake
and fall,
I'd take away the gun and the duck you shot

but if pneumonia had to be,
I'd give you company for the three months
you spent in hospital.

I'd give you long trousers for your first job,
so your skin wouldn't stick to the whitened seat
delivering milk on the frosty mornings.

I'd leave the copper kettle
you bought before your marriage
on the Kathleen Mavourneen from the ESB

so you might pass it on to me
along with all your stories.

First Born
for Matilda

You said she broke your heart
from her first breath,
from her first wail

in your frightened arms.
You could see, you said, the day ahead
when she would leave you;

eighteen years in the blink of an eye.
Suppose, I said, *oh brother,*
she broke your heart open

with such a tender love
it almost killed you,
so you could love not only her

but all of us.

Rainy Days

for my godchild Julia

I'm sure the gods have children
and on rainy days in heaven
they let them out to play on earth.

See them sliding down the rainbow
at the speed of light, poppy seeds
spilling from their pockets,

or racing pell-mell through the forest
flashing silver undersides of leaf,
the jingle of money and high-pitched shrieks.

The older ones like painting landscapes
in unusual blues, indigos and violets
with a glint of gold.

The godly teens lean out the stratospheric windows,
puffing smoke rings from their dad's cigars
into clouds of mare's-tails, and a whole circus

fills the sky. Their favourite game is tickling
babies while they nap, and they wink and shush
them up as if to say

let's keep our secret secret
for another rainy day.

On the road

I often find myself
in other lives
I could have led
quite easily –
generic towns,
roads I do not know
but seem familiar.

That bungalow, two cars,
two jobs, two kids, two dogs.

It may happen yet
that I wake up in a bed
with a man I've known
for years by smell.

I dreamed of my children last night,
window-shopping in O'Connell street,
my arms around them.

My boy, my girl.
So clearly mine that when I woke
I searched the room.
Wherever I left them
I must let them wait
and return to earth
without them.

Sweeping

i
A woman is sweeping the beach
at Gloucester and she is not mad.

She never explains who employs her
or what her rate of pay,

but I suspect she is part
of a movement of brushes

worldwide, whose force
may yet become a storm.

Sweeping
in memory of Maria Reiche, Nasca, Peru

ii
Only a woman would
sweep for fifty years
the fifty miles of lines.

Piling up the dark baked stones
on either side
so the lighter gypsum soil

revealed the monkey's curling tail,
the humming bird, the whale,
the condor's outstretched wings

across the desert in scorching heat.
Not just swept but measured,
inch by inch, the ancient maps

left by parched Paracas long ago,
who danced the lines in worship,

swept those clear blue skies
with tearless eyes
to make the rain clouds bloom.

Feamainn Dearg
after Hafiz

If god were here
she'd be a swathe of feamainn dearg
loosely attached to a green rock
shining this way and that
teaching us about the weather.

If god were here she'd be
a pair of faded denims,
with two pockets front and back
– one each for fire, water, earth and air –
that I could slip into and revel.

If god were my beloved
I would laugh uncontrollably
and make such a drunken nuisance of myself,
she would have to lean down
and comb me into her hair.

Letters to my Ego

Dear Ego,

Cosetted
in our castle,

hidden from the world,
you keep me

like gold bars
in a time-delayed safe.

Thank you for
the tarnished darkness,

the ashes of boredom.
Through a chink of sun

in the stone fortress,
I count the cost

of my lack of courage.

Yours truly,
M.

Dear Mary,

You have forgotten
you made me
to protect you,

to defend you,
and befriend you
in your wretched state

of separation.
Who cast you out
into the bitter world?

Your ego?

E.

Dear Ego,

I don't remember
choosing any of this –

my shipwrecked birth,
being carried to the castle

like Cuchulainn when he fought
the deathless sea.

Are you my Emer
who must renounce my love forever?

Who is the keeper,
who the kept?

Yours truly?
M.

Dear Mary,

I haven't had a day off
in years. You are not
easy to live with,

always in a mood,
demanding drama
and applause.

On retirement I'd like
to drowse, like an old dog
in the winter sun.

E.

Dear E,

Why are you dressed in black?
That hat is pure Dickens,

the whiskers are out of date.
Are you Doctor Foster

going to Gloucester
in a shower of rain?

Best wishes,
Yours truly,
M.

Dear M,

I have no sense of humour,
but changing clothes is simple.
Tell me what to wear;

a sailor's uniform
or cleric's robe,
the head butler's gear?

Is my job description changing
from a gaoler to a doorman?
Am I to go on special training?

E.

Dear E,

Like the grey heron
knee-deep in a fast river,

I am standing still.
Give me wings to swim.

Yours truly,
M.

Dear M,

I know about your search
for *sruth na cainte.*

On the night of the new moon,
let the darkness shine
through closed eyes,

let the emptiness
fill you

from
Within.

Dear E,

I dreamt we were to marry,
barefoot in my green suit,

hoping I'd recognise you
at the altar.

Yours truly,
M.

Dear M,

We are already yoked
like oxen,
though we pull apart at times

and drag the other
to the field –
the plough is just for show.

Resistance doesn't work
and there is nothing like
the familiar trawl

on uneven earth.
Up and down the same
beloved furrow.

E.

Dear E,

I want out of every furrow.
We are not beasts of burden.

I long for freedom,
though I don't know what it is.

Let my own fierce passion come
and carry me away.

Yours truly,
M.

Dear M,

We've had a past,
I'm offering you
a future, time is ticking …

You are the centre
of my worries, your
safety foremost

in an unsafe world.

E.

Dear E,

You are an impostor,
with your past and future.

I want what you
can never give –

peace from your incessant
talk, your bitchy running

commentary, your wind-ups
and your put-downs,

I want to be thoughtless,
I am,

not yours truly,
M.

Dear M,

How have we come to this
misunderstanding, that you have turned
a deaf ear to all my warnings?

Is there someone else to guide you
in these frightening times? Who knows
you better than me?

E.

Dear E,

Yes I have a new adviser,
who was with me all along,

who could never get a word in
except on rare occasions

when I'd slip into a reverie
and you were gone.

I'm not asking you to leave
after all we've been through,

consider it a lifelong lease
or early retirement,

drowsing like my old dog
in the winter sun.

M.

Pins and Needles

When did we start kneeling,
crouching over polished pews in church
on Sunday mornings? At home,
keeling into musty cushions,

muffling our *Hail Marys*
at auctioneering speed,
searching through the torn upholstery
for biscuit crumbs and pennies.

Jesus told me straight.
He said, *Get off your knees.*
I laughed and cried through pins and needles
and followed fully clothed
into the white blue sea.

Old Testament Times
for Joe Duffy

One said
It was Adam and Eve in the garden, Joe.
Not Adam and Steve.

Two said
Let Jesus into your heart, Joe.
It'll all be cured.

Three said
And a man shall not lie with a man, Joe.
The Bible says.

Four said
They're all gay in the seminary, Joe.
Every single one of them.

And Joe said
Does the Catholic Church know about that?

I said
We don't live in Old Testament times, Joe.
Women don't get stoned any more, Joe,
except on their home-grown grass.

And Joe said
Next caller please.

Six said
I'm gay and I'm proud, Joe.
And I still go to mass, Joe.
And no one will stop me, Joe.

And what does the church think of that?
said Joe

Seven said
I'm gay and I'm married, Joe.
And me children don't know, Joe.
A priest said I'd grow out of it.
Me husband's a good man, Joe.
But I don't know.

Eight said
I think she should stay with her man, Joe.
Think of the children, Joe.
And she's made her bed.

Nine said
I met a fella once, Joe.
And he was going to kill himself, Joe.
On account of being gay.

And Joe said
I'm way over time folks.
That's all for today.

Eve's Last Letter

Dear Adam,
Along with the decree nisi and absolute
I'm sending you a letter

and hope you will consider
my humble pride in you and hatred also.
I blamed you for loving Cain.
I blamed myself for loving Abel more.

We didn't teach them well.
Cain engineered Abel's disappearance
before he fled the farm,

repeating our disgrace
as we fled the garden long ago.
But I don't regret the apple,
our years spent on the run.

I want you to remember me young
when I was the only one for you,
before you disappeared in basement bars

conspiring with the ignorant.
Had you really no idea of your greatness?
Our sons are gone, our daughters too
and we have nothing left to lose or spend.

But I do not want my freedom
if only *I* am free.
Adam can you hear me?

Can we start again?
Though we are old and weary,
is there something left
to start again?

Waiting for a Miracle

I wish I could go
to Gortahork
or take a bus from Puno
across the Andes

without the ancestors screaming
oh my god, oh my god, oh my god.

The poor in the dark
dreaming of summer,
the Bridge of Tears ahead.

But I'm waiting
for a miracle,
wondering too
if the luxury of thought
is wasted on the past,
the unseen lives,
the unheard cries
that plague me.

The heart has many cages
and few escapes:
the beating
thuds of loss;
a shovelful of clay
on a hollow box.

Where can I find a field
free of sorrow?

The Final Miracle

Lazarus lay in a coma
not dead at all, though

his heartbeat was imperceptible,
the body gone cold.

I prayed at the door
saying, *Father I don't know*

about this. It's up to you,
but it will certainly up the ante

and Lazarus doesn't want
this world or his mother's grieving,

his sister's love is not the lover
he wants now.

Whose will is strongest?
Another miracle might kill me.

Glencar

Today the lake was pewter grey.
Dark yellow silverweed dotted

the ditch. A blur of ragged robin
stitched under the sycamore hazel

canopy of early June. I've never
seen the road so lovely.

I've changed my mind about
the world. It's paradise

or at the very least, heaven
under construction.

The wind picks up as I
turn the corner. There are

only two cars at the entrance
to the waterfall. After all

these years I realise
I'm not a visitor;
I live here, I belong.

Christ at Carrowkeel

When Christ was on his world tour
He stopped at Carrowkeel
prayed in the upper cairn
as the setting solstice rays
met him in the chamber.

He blessed the mystic engineers
and called them forth
to calibrate an opening
where his presence
could be summoned
and he could slip
through the silver quartz
like sunlight.

Beyond Words
for Leland Bardwell

1.
I heard something from your soul
and I drank there
that ruby dawn

and came out black,
not with grief,
but dark beside your light.

Let me trouble you only two or three days.
In the book of my life
there's only one page left;

in a small lined copybook
I am writing my last poems,
my last loving glance.

That field made me weep;
the river Rye of my youth;
a burnt-out house …

and beyond words,
a ragged jacket,
pockets torn and empty,

spent with endless
seeking, always drunk
on love's cheap wine.

Here on the last rock
in the Atlantic,
I have one word left

and I'm not using it
just yet. I am waiting
for the ruby dawn

then *my* days
will lose their dayness
and slip my grasp.

2.
That word you are keeping
will be the last one to see you,

but I can't accept
that death comes home like that,

rowing, rowing through
the lonesome wake.

Forget yourself in passionate song;
call up the whales with Port na bPúcaí.

Your hourglass may be upended,
though the body cannot pour,

the full *you* slips from the bottle;
a genie uncorked and weightless,

free to stay in the river forever
or find your way to the sea.

3.
We are poles apart
when we can't pay
attention.

It's the heart has ears
not the head –
or if it has

they only listen
to the dull sound
of trouble.

4.
We both are dying;
neither here nor there.
I don't know how
to take you to the station,

or which one.
I only know
I will not let you
go alone.

5.
Some of the storms were fierce
that spewed out into night;
bitter lees, a dark stain
that cut us off for days
until they blew themselves out
and we left our fixed positions

for the sake of peace.
Beyond words, I know
that every single thing's
in order, though
I neither see nor hear
the angels, they're always near.

I've been picking berries
from the rowan trees
in Lissadell
since the thunder moon
has come and gone.
I want to make a wine

to set the heart singing
like the violin that has
forgiven every wound
wrought by others.
I want to make a wine
that sets the heart free.

6.
Yes, I listen to whatever makes you talk
or stop what you are doing.

I listen in my silent heart
to the gaps in sound

as you breathe out
and before you reach

for breath again.
Sometimes the only place

we can agree
is beyond words.

7.
Cormorants gather,
showing off

their wheeling loops
and delving depths.

But we are looking
at the iceberg cloud

exposed on the cliffs
of the heart across the bay,

bearing down on
Cloonagh and Lislarry.

The long boat parked
on Seagull Street is not forgotten,

but overgrown with oxeye daisies
and probably rotten.

There's been a parade of ghosts
all evening to the skull of a house.

We'll never get
to Inishmurray now

except on wings.